THE
GREAT
REPLACEMENT

Strategic End Time Intercessory Warfare

Strategies for overpowering the enemy by becoming God's
Atmosphere Changers and bringing His presence into the earth

Diane White
D.Min. BCMMHC

ISBN 978-1-63630-910-1 (Paperback)
ISBN 978-1-63630-911-8 (Digital)

Covenant Books, Inc.
11661 Hwy 707
Murrells Inlet, SC 29576
www.covenantbooks.com

CONTENTS

INTRODUCTION

This book is written for the saints of God. It is an illumination of scriptures that we are familiar with and an invitation for all of us to come up a little higher. The scriptures are ones that we have read in the past that contain the secrets of an end-time spiritual warfare strategy. God is calling us to the greatest intercessory movement that has ever existed. He is calling us all into action if we are willing to accept the challenge and the assignment.

As the one that was chosen to write this, I have by no means accomplished all that God requires. I too am on the journey, with an even greater level of responsibility as I pen all that God is speaking to my spirit. You will find the book addressed to *we* and *us* for this very reason. My prayer is for all the Body of Christ (me included) that:

- We will lean on God like never before so that we can accomplish what He desires to do in our lives.
- We will be the army of God that does great exploits for the Kingdom of God.
- We will unite, as never before to do the will of God in these last and evil days.

As a pastor in the intercity, a counselor dealing with those with mental illness and/or addictions, an African American female, and a daughter of the Most High God for over forty years, I have had many opportunities to see the multiple changes in mankind and the vast warfare that ensue as mankind tries to daily live life. I myself, though a product of a two-parent, middle-class home whose marriage lasted until death, was born into conflict as an African American in a country that doubted my potential.

My journey continued down a road of conflict as I accepted the call to be a female pastor. However, unlike many women called to this position, I had the luxury of partnering with my husband, the bishop, to do ministry. As a counselor, I have had the awesome opportunity of walking alongside women who have survived trauma, mental illness, violence, addiction, and the stigma that the church places on such individuals with these struggles. My point is that I am no stranger to conflict, hatred, unacceptance, and the associated warfare. The truth is that most people are not stranger to any of these things either.

As a little girl, I remembered Martin Luther King, Joe Lewis, and all the others who lead people of color and their supporters to peacefully protest against the injustices of that time. They were strategic and adamant about protesting in peace and upholding that stance of peace even when attacked, beaten, and arrested. To be heard was their mission, but peace was also their mission, "Can you hear my protest to the status quo if I bring it to you calm and in peace?" Unfortunately, I have also had the opportunity to witness those who felt peaceful protest didn't change things so they concluded that destruction would get them the attention and the platform needed to address injustices. But as we continue on in the year of 2020, we see that neither peace nor destruction was able to eliminate the hate that fuels the systemic injustices that continue.

As a woman of prayer, I began to seek God for what He would do in light of where we are today. We are now nearing the end of 2020 and I have never seen anything like it before. Blatant hatred, televised murder with no real consequences, the conspiracy of lies, and deception, and yet multiple races are now coming together to peacefully protest. There is still some destruction, but the truth is that those that destroy are attempting to silence, by their actions, the ones asking, "Can you hear my protest if I bring it to you calmly, peacefully, and in solidarity?" I'm encouraged by the united effort of all the peaceful protestors but God keeps dealing with me about more has to be done if we want to see a real change.

All of the efforts of the unified protest are good naturally, but God said to me, "What about the spiritual fight?" After all hate, confusion, lies, fear and all the darkness are all spirits. Is nonviolent civil resistance successful? History has shown that nonviolent civil resistance is far more successful in creating broad-based change than violent campaigns have been. However, what we are looking at in this end-time is not about changing the thoughts of people. Instead, what is needed is a change in the hearts of the people.

CHAPTER 1

A Change of Heart

What exactly is in the hearts of some of the people? With each day of new releases in the news, we see hatred displayed in a spirit of prejudice, witchcraft displayed by the spirits of manipulation, and deception and religion displayed in a spirit of pride and the lack of compassion. Every day the darkness in the hearts of some mankind is over-shadowing the light in the hearts of those who profess to love God. How can the darkness overpower the light when any flicker of light should dispel darkness? Could it be that those that profess to love God don't carry the light of God? What is really going on here?

How do the people of God, deal with all that continues to take place each day. First, I think we have to go back to the beginning in Genesis 1:26–28 (AMP):

> God said, Let Us [Father, Son, and Holy Spirit] make mankind in Our image, after Our likeness and let them have complete authority over the fish of the sea, the birds of the air, the [tame] beasts and over all of the earth, and over everything that creeps upon the earth. So God created man in His own image, in the image and likeness of God He created him, male and female He created them. And God bless them and said to them, Be fruitful, multiply and fill the earth,

and subdue it [using all its vast resources in the service of God and man], and have dominion over the fish of the sea, the birds of the air, and over every living creature that moves upon the earth.

Here we find that God created all mankind in His image and gave mankind dominion over the beast of the earth. We were made with a plan in place. We were supposed to be in God's likeness and His image, so He gave us dominion over the earth. We were to use the resource of this earth in the service of God and man. It was about the community not about selfishness and self-promotion. He did not give us dominion over each other because we were all made in His image. Any mankind or womankind that would come after the creation of Adam would have the potential to be in the image of God.

I say potential because as Adam decided to take his own route we all have the ability to not go God's way yet we have within us the potential to operate in the image of God if we choose to do so. In choosing to do things God's way, we choose to operate in His image which is attached to the dominion and authority over the earth. When the people of God don't operate in dominion and authority over the earth there is chaos and darkness. So there is chaos and darkness because the people of God cannot access dominion and authority until they walk in the image of God. Unless we can love like God loves, a love that is available to any and all we can never look like Him.

Is there any encouragement from belonging to Christ? Any comfort from His Love? Any fellowship together in the Spirit? Are your hearts tender and compassionate? Then make me truly happy by agreeing whole-heartedly with each other, loving one another, and working together with one mind and purpose. Don't be selfish, don't try to impress others. Be humble, thinking of others as better than yourselves. Don't look out only for your own interest, but take an interest in others, too. You must have the same attitude that Christ Jesus had. (Philippians 2:1–5 NLT)

A new commandment I give unto you, That ye love one another, as I have loved you, that ye also love one another. By this shall all men know that ye are my disciples if you have love one to another. (John 13:34–35)

God began to show me that love was the key to authority. God is love and that is part of His character and only when we can operate in His love will He give us authority. We are to walk in love and then we can walk in authority. To the extent that our love is limited so will our authority be limited. Everything must be done in love; otherwise, He cannot trust us with authority. Even when you are upset with someone, if we walk in love we are expected to encounter them in a loving way to address a conflict. Not to seek to hurt them, harm them, or kill them. We mankind operate outside of God's image, and we have replaced authority with power. We seek to manipulate and overpower and dominate because there is no real authority.

Year after year of chaos has caused our land to be broken. Families are broken, marriages are broken, neighborhoods, cities, states, and our nation are all broken. Chaos has broken every aspect of our being so the people are physically, mentally, emotionally, and spiritually broken. As a counselor, I encounter those who suffer from generations of hurt and brokenness. I have discovered that many people are completely broken, and yet the truth is that everyone has some area of brokenness that they are trying to cover up; people cover up with beauty, material possession, money, or power.

God has allowed me to see past the false demeanor that is presented in an attempt to cover up so that no one knows what is really going on inside. People have perfected the ability to appear alright when everything is really upside down in their life. And this is also true for those of us who come together to worship God and profess that we are His disciples. If a change of heart is to take place it is the Body of Christ that has to be the first partakers of this change. Without us first changing, we can't expect the masses to change.

CHAPTER 2

A Healing for the Land

The Bible provides a scripture that tells us what can be done to heal a broken land. This is a well know scripture that is commonly used in speeches just before or after people gather together with signs and catchy chants as they march in solidarity for a particular cause. If not then certainly on Sunday morning when the preacher steps into the pulpit and tries to calm the pains of injustice felt by those sitting in the pews.

> If my people, who are called by My name, shall humble themselves, pray, seek, crave and require of necessity My face and turn from their wicked ways, then will I hear from heaven, forgive their sin and heal their land. (2 Chronicles 7:14 AMP)

This is the commonly cited scripture and I believe our answer is in it. But why haven't things gotten better in the world? Why are things worse? I believe that the hindrance is not that we don't know what this scripture is saying but the hindrance is in that the people of God do not understand the depth of what is required of us for God to heal our land.

I submit to you that the beginning of our spiritual protest (which I will talk about in more detail later) begins here. We have to hear the mind of God and what He is telling us in this scripture to begin to counteract what the enemy had unleashed into the atmosphere.

My People Called by My Name

These instructions are not addressed to those who don't know God. He specifically lets us know that you must have already confessed to Jesus Christ and have accepted that you are part of His people and also called by His name. This is addressed to the body of Christ. The body of Christ, however, has been so attached to their churches, their organization, and what can be acquired personally from these attachments. In my observation, we, the body of Christ have forgotten the original plan and covenant of Genesis 1:26–28.

Our forgetfulness has caused us to veer off course. Being off course has gotten us to a place where we are trying to please a man without considering whether or not we are operating in the image and likeness of God. In moving with the crowd, we have stepped away from the dominion and now operate in control. We, the church, need to reflect back on the covenant God made with Adam that was lost by his disobedience but retrieved for our benefit by Jesus's obedience to die on the cross. We have the opportunity to walk in dominion and authority but we must be His people. We should look, think, and act like Him.

Humble Ourselves

How do we humble ourselves when for most of us we have felt the need to show others what we can do and how anointed we may be in comparison to all the others who claimed to have the same calling. Just like on the job where we seek to be promoted by our performance, we do the same thing in the church. Our acts of service should be nothing but what we do out of our heart not considering what we can acquire from that service. The problem with worldliness is that the church for years has always spoken of it as a way of looking and dressing but worldliness has been able to slip right into the church because we overlooked the thoughts and attitudes that constituted and fuel worldly behavior.

Competition is a worldly thought pattern that has no right in the church. Where competition exists humility is considered a weakness. On the job, you are encouraged to promote your strengths and not talk about your weakness. Anyone who won't toot their own horn out of humility is expected and will for the most part be overlooked. Because humble people in the workplace are considered weak, people who considered themselves strong personalities seek to control these individuals.

So what does humility look like in the church? First of all it is a stance of strength understanding that whatever you can do is because of the God that you are connected to and not about your own abilities. It is about not always having to shine but letting other shine. Taking the back seat and not having to be in the forefront and not having to be the one in control all the time. Jesus gave us an example of humility in John 13:3–8 (AMP):

> [That] Jesus, knowing (fully aware) that the Father had put everything into His hands, and that He had come from God and was [now] returning to God. Got up from supper, took off His garments, and taking a [servant's] towel, He fastened it around His waist. Then He poured water into the washbasin and began to wash the disciples' feet and to wipe them with the [servant's] towels with which He was girded. When he came to Simon Peter, [Peter} said to Him, Lord, are my feet to be washed by You? [Is it for You to wash my feet?] Jesus said to him, You do not understand now what I am doing, but you will understand later on. Peter said to Him. You shall never wash my feet! Jesus answered him, unless I wash you, you have no part with (*in) Me [you have no share in companionship with Me].

In the day and time of this scripture, the washing of feet was a servant's job. A leader was never to take on this responsibility. It was considered demeaning and below a leader. But the scripture clearly states that Jesus knew who He was and that everything was in His hands, yet he humbled himself to do a minimal act so that we could understand that humility is not an act of weakness but an act of strength. Jesus also let us know that he was doing this for our later admonishment and that unless we could get with His way of thinking and acting, we would not be a part of Him.

Pray, Seek, Crave, and Require of Necessity My Face

Every Christians soon learn that the way we talk to God is in pray and meditation, giving Him the opportunity to speak back to us about His desires for our life. As a pastor and intercessor, I have observed that our least attended yet the most powerful service is prayer service. I still have not been able to determine why this service has the least people in attendance. Perhaps it is because there is no opportunity to be at the forefront or on the stage. In this service, it is just you and God in a community setting, yet having your own personal intimate discussion with God.

Getting to know Him better, as well as getting a clear picture of ourselves, all happens in prayer. This is not about coming before God to ask for things and making our requests known. Don't get me wrong, there is nothing wrong with making our requests to the only one who can fulfill them. However, these requests are seeking His hand, wanting Him to give you something. But the scripture says to seek His face. Seeking His face is such an intimate encounter because it is in this process that we learn about who He is and who we are to be in Him.

Real prayer will get you that close to God, face-to-face, right in front of Him where the mystery of Him will be exposed to you and also where nothing about you is hidden from Him. That might be an unsettling thought but in reality, nothing about us is hidden from Him anyway. But the awesome thing is that, if you purposefully seek God's face, what He is about and the path that you must take will be revealed to you. God hides nothing from those who seek His face, who long and crave to be in His presence and to have an intimate conversation.

It is in the face of God that we find the secret place; the place spoken of in Psalm 91. This scripture clearly states the benefits of being in the secret place of the Most High. But, where there are benefits, there are also prerequisites. These prerequisites are something that has to be done or a position that you must be in to reap the benefits. The benefit is the safety of abiding in the presence of God. Abiding suggests that there is no going in and out but that one has to make their home and set up residence in the presence of God. In this place, there is deliverance from snares set up by the enemy to defeat you, deliverance from pestilence and from destruction.

My personal favorite benefit is in Psalm 91:7, which says, "A thousand may fall at your side and ten thousand at your right hand; but it shall not come near you." It grounds me so that I am not delusional, expecting that I will never experience upsets but that in the midst of the upsets, others may feel it and be overtaken by it, but in God's presence, I will see it but not experience the effects of it.

I know the question comes to mind, "How can a person be present for their daily responsibilities of taking care of a home, going to a job, and just doing their everyday duties?" The next question is whether a person would have to isolate themselves in a room and never come out, in order to abide in the presence of God. If we look to Jesus as our example, we will notice that he took time with people and socialized with them to the point that the Pharisee criticized him because of all the time He spent with those categorized as a sinner. But He was in the presence of God and being about the business of God. Jesus knew and demonstrated to us, how to be open to the people and connect with them while still be connected to God. I have personally found that even in my constant movement, God can be in my mind and in my thoughts. As I remain in a state of peace, I'm in His presence.

Though in reference to the desire to give finances in support of ministry makes a good point that whenever we have a desire to do anything out of our love for God, He is there to help us complete what is in our heart to do. (2 Corinthians 8:12)

For if there is first a willing mind, it is accepted according to what one has and not according to what he does not have. (2 Corinthians 8:12)

Jesus said unto him, If thou canst believe, all things are possible to him that believeth. (Mark 9:23)

All it takes is for us to first believe that it is possible to abide in God's presence and then be willing to pursue the challenge of abiding in His presence. Then wait and watch as God helps you to do just what you desire to do. I have found that the desire to do this gives God the open door to makes it possible and meet your desire.

Thou hast given him his heart's desires and have not withheld the request of his lips. (Psalm 21:2)

He will fulfill the desire of those who fear Him; He also will hear their cry and save them. (Psalm 145:19)

There are some things we can desire that will only bless our carnal man, and yet God provides the answer to that request. But when the desire we present to God is that we want to spend more time with Him, He will answer that request. God's desire is to spend more time with us as well and it blesses His heart when He finds out that we feel the same.

Turn from Their Wicked Ways

> The earth is the Lord's and everything in it. The world and all its people belong to him; For he laid the earth's foundation on the seas and built it on the ocean depths. Who may climb the mountain of the Lord? Who may stand in his holy place? Only those whose hands and hearts are pure, who do not worship idols and never tell lies. They will receive the Lord's blessing and have a right relationship with God their savior. Such people may seek you and worship in your presence, O God of Jacob. (Psalm 24:1–6 NLT)

Turning from their wicked ways is the third hurdle that God's people will have to overcome. The hardest thing for a religious person to admit is that they have wicked ways. Part of the problem is that our idea of wicked is tainted by what things we still like to do and that we have not fully surrendered over to God. The thought is, *If I struggle with this thing, it is not that bad because God knows my heart and I love Him.* And don't let me be active in ministry yet have a thing that I struggle with because even when I do something that is not right because I love God and am a Christian doing a work for Him, I get a pass.

Psalm 24 states that only those with pure hands and hearts and who don't worship idols and tell lies will be able to come into the holy mountain where God is present. What microscope do we put our hands and heart under to determine if there is any impurity on our hands or in our hearts? It is not possible nor is it prudent to evaluate the condition of our own heart. Psalm 44:21 says, "Shall not God search this out? For he knoweth the secrets of the heart." So God has to help us in making the determination of the purity of our hands and heart.

Next, Psalm 24 speaks of not worshipping idols. The enemy has gotten very creative in his developing of idols in our lives. Idols can be our children, spouse, job, material item, our ministry, and/or our titles, our education level obtained, and any addiction that we struggle with. Basically, it is any things that take your attention away from God and what He wants you to do. It is the thing that you can't do without. Lastly, it specifically says that liars cannot come into God's presence. Of all the sins that man can commit this scripture mentions liars, which shows how serious God is about what elements, emotions, and attitudes are brought into His presence. Most of us don't even think about a lie as something that will take us out of the presence of God. But God has given us specific instruction about what He will not allow to be brought into His presence.

Our idea of wicked has to be the same as God's idea of wicked. Philippians 2:5 says, "Let this mind be in you, which was also in Christ Jesus." We have to be willing to admit that any wicked action, deed, or thought is sin in God's eyes. Even the horrible things that we don't speak about but are deep in our heart have to be dealt with such as:

- hatred based on prejudice
- unfairness based on favoritism
- lies based on deceptive acts or omissions of facts

When we hate no matter what reason created the hate; when we treat one person better than another; when we tell what is commonly known as a *little white lie*; all these acts are wicked ways in God's eyes. That is why it is so important to seek His face. It is those intimate moments with God where He will show you what needs to be changed and then empower you to make the changes. As 2 Corinthians 8:12 says, all we need is a willing mind and God will work with what we bring to Him in those intimate moments. The presence of the Lord has the ability to change us, to cleanse us, and to take us out of bondage.

This is the message we heard from Jesus and now declare to you. God is light and there is no darkness in him at all. So we are lying if we say we have fellowship with God but go on living in spiritual darkness, we are not practicing the truth. But if we are living in the light as God is the light, then we have fellowship with each other and the blood of Jesus his Son cleanses us from all sin. If we claim we have no sin, we are only fooling ourselves and not living in the truth. But if we confess our sins to him, he is faithful and just to forgive us our sins and to cleanse us from all wickedness. If we claim we have not sinned we are calling God a liar and showing that his word has no place in our hearts. (1 John 9:5–10 NLT)

As we get closer and closer to God in our moments of seeking His face, we move closer into His image and likeness. In His face, we will understand His mind and the things He perceives as wickedness. We have to be willing to get naked before Him. We can't hide behind our education, money, or titles. We have to come clean and allow Him to heal us. When the people of God who have been given dominion are healed, then the land will be healed, as God promised in 2 Chronicles 7:14.

Getting through this process is just the beginning of the strategy of engaging in a spiritual protest. It is just the beginning of what I call the Great Replacement. The spiritual place of God's people that will dictate whether the spirits operating in the world today will continue to operate or will be replaced by the Kingdom of God and His principles.

CHAPTER 3

Taking Part in the Spiritual Protest

Spiritual Protest

What is a spiritual protest? As I was looking at the days and days of protests happening all over the world, several things were very clear about what it took to have such an event. First, for all those people to come together in unity, especially during a pandemic, there had to be a unified cause that they all felt was worthy of the time and effort it took to protest. Secondly, there had to be an organization so that the various areas of protest would be unified. Lastly, there had to be expectations that were expressed to those involved so that the protest would remain peaceful. Then as we were in prayer, the term spiritual protest dropped into my spirit as we asked God to show us what could be done to really address the problems of today.

A Cause Worthy of Coming Together to Protest

The overwhelming essence of the consistent reports of hatred in actions or in spoken words, along with the lies and deceptions, and the chaos of the pandemic has created spiritual darkness in the atmosphere. The infusion of all of these things coming together at one time certainly should be a wake-up call for the church. God's people should come together and ask themselves:

- How did this happen on our watch?
- Were we being watchful at all?
- What went wrong and how can we change it?
- What must we do to make sure there is a change?

God's people will have to come together and agree that there is a problem that is naturally seen but is the direct manifestation of a spiritual problem. We must be organized in our efforts, not fighting over who is in charge because our general is the Lord God, mighty in battle. And finally, we need to be clear on the part that we must play and stay within those boundaries as the Joel 2 army.

> Blow the trumpet in Zion, and sound an alarm in My holy mountain; let all the inhabitants of the land tremble! For the day of the Lord is coming. For it is at hand; A day of darkness and gloominess.; A day of clouds and thick darkness.; Like the morning clouds spread over the mountains. A people come, great and strong, the like of whom has never been: Nor will there ever by any such after them. Even for many successive generations.
>
> A fire devours before them, and behind them a flame burns. The land is like the Garden of Eden before them; and behind them a desolate wilderness; Surely nothing shall escape them. Their appearance is like the appearance of horses; and like swift steeds, so they run. With a noise like chariots, over the mountaintops they leap, like the noise of a flaming fire that devours the stubble, like a strong people set in battle array.
>
> Before them the people writhe in pain; all faces are drained of color. They run like mighty

men, they climb the wall like men of war; every one marches in formation. And they do not break ranks. They do not push one another; every one marches in his own column. Though they lunge between the weapons, they are not cut down. They run on the wall; they climb into the houses, they enter at the windows like a thief.

The earth quakes before them, the heavens tremble; the sun and moon grow dark, and the stars diminish their brightness. The Lord gives voice before His army, for His camp is very great; for strong is the One who executes His word. For the day of the Lord is great and very terrible; who can endure it?

Now therefore, says the Lord, Turn to Me with all your heart, with fasting, with weeping, and with mourning. So rend your heart, and not your garments; return to the Lord your God. For He is gracious and merciful, slow to anger and of great kindness; and He relents from doing harm. Who knows if He will turn and relent; and leave a blessing behind Him-a grain offering and a drink offering for the Lord your God?

Blow the trumpet in Zion, consecrate a fast, call a sacred assembly; gather the people, sanctify the congregation. Assemble the elders, gather the children and nursing babes; let the bridegroom go out from his chamber and the bride from her dressing room. Let the priests who minister to the Lord, weep between the porch and the altar; let them say, "Spare Your people O Lord, and do not give Your heritage to reproach, that the nations should rule over them. Why should they say among the peoples, where is their God"?

Then the Lord will be zealous for His land, and pity the people. The Lord will answer and

> say to His people, behold I will send you grain
> and new wine and oil. And you will be satisfied
> by them; I will no longer make you a reproach
> among the nations. (Joel 2:1–19)

The church must be aware that for every natural battle there is a corresponding spiritual battle that is simultaneously occurring. So while there is a unified front that is protesting to see things change, we, God's people have to follow God's instructions by doing our own battle. It requires a change in us so that we can prepare for the spiritual protest. We cannot vacillate between a natural protest and a spiritual one. We must stay focus on God's method of doing war. And as we do, we will see the tapestry of the world changed. God's army will cause things to burn, the earth to quake, and will cause people to turn back to the Lord, all with our prayers and declarations.

> For though we walk in the flesh, we do not
> war according to the flesh; for the weapons of our
> warfare are not carnal but mighty in God for pull-
> ing down strongholds, casting down arguments
> and every high thing that exalts itself against the
> knowledge of God, bringing every thought into
> captivity to the obedience of Christ; and being
> ready to punish all disobedience when your obe-
> dience is fulfilled. (2 Corinthians 10:3–6)

Our weapons are mighty in God and cannot be operated outside of Him. These weapons are designed to pull down the stronghold. The hatred, prejudice, injustice, and darkness are all strongholds that keep those affected by them in bondage. These bondages cannot be broken through conversation and protest. The change that has to happen in the hearts of the people in bondage has to be done by weapons designed by God to bring thoughts into captivity and to create within the person the desire to be obedient to God and His principals. But we, the church, have to see that we are only ready to deal with others' disobedience when we ourselves are completely obedient to not just some of the word but to all of the word.

The initial preparation to operate these weapons of warfare starts when we daily operate in the image and likeness of God, which is our reasonable service. It is the expectations that we must implore in order for our spiritual protest to remain spiritual and not gravitate to a natural protest when the spiritual change has not completely manifested in the natural realm.

> I appeal to you therefore, brethren, and beg of you, in view of [all] the mercies of God, to make a decisive dedication of your bodies [presenting all your members and faculties] as a living sacrifice, holy (devoted, consecrated) and well pleasing to God, which is your reasonable (rational, intelligent) service and spiritual worship. Do not be conformed to this world (this age), [fashioned after and adapted to its external, superficial customs], but be transformed (changed) by the [entire] renewal of your mind [by its new ideals and its new attitude], so that you may prove [for yourselves], what is the good and acceptable and perfect will of God, even the thing which is good and acceptable and perfect [in His sight for you]. (Romans 12:1–2 AMP)

So what is the key aspect of a spiritual protest? It is the ability of God's people to habitually live in God's presence to the point that we bring Him along with us everywhere we go; Thereby allowing His presence to change the atmosphere and the hearts of the people and to destroy the strongholds that have them bound.

> Blessed are the undefiled in the way, who walk in the law of the Lord. Blessed are those who keep His testimonies, who seek Him with the whole heart! They also do no iniquity; they

> walk in His ways. You have commanded us to
> keep Your precepts diligently. Oh, that my ways
> were directed to keep Your statutes. Then I would
> not be ashamed when I look into all Your com-
> mandments. (Psalm 119:1–6)

The change in us, God's people, is what is needed to change the world. We need to stop putting down our religion to deal with conflict. Instead, we should be carriers of God's presence that will be manifested in our character. We must implore the weapons designed by God to be used to nullify the darkness of conflicts. Only when we have readied ourselves to do this can we be used by God, as atmosphere changers, for the Great Replacement. What is the Great Replacement that God is seeking for those to avail themselves to be a participant in? It is the greatest intercessory move that has ever taken place.

> The people of the land have used oppres-
> sions, committed robbery and mistreated the
> poor and needy; and they wrongfully oppress the
> stranger. So I sought for a man among them who
> would make a wall, and stand in the gap before
> Me on behalf of the land that I should not destroy
> it; but I found no one. (Ezekiel 22:29–30)

God is looking for not just one person but many who will commit to replacing the hatred in the world with overpowering love; to replace darkness in the world with light, His light; to replace the lies and deceptions in the world with God's truth, and to replace the conflict and chaos in the world with the peace of God. Those who choose to make this commitment must not allow situations or circumstances to change the cause for which they stand. God's people must come to a place where they bring the Kingdom of God to earth by living in the atmosphere of the kingdom while residing on the earth. When we become carriers of the kingdom of God like Jesus was, our presence carrying God's presence will change the world. At that point, we have become God's Atmosphere Changers.

> Let God arise, let His enemies be scattered; let those also who hate Him flee before Him. As smoke is driven away; as wax melts before the fire, so let the wicked perish at the presence of God. (Psalm 68:12)

Let me be clear here. Where this scripture talks about the enemy and uses the pronoun "them," it is not talking about people but the spirits that fight a move of God. These spirits will be scattered as God arises in the lives of His people. We are never to attack the person but we are to take captive the spirit that is driving them to do evil acts.

CHAPTER 4

Replacing the Spirit of Hate

The only way to overpower and replace hate is by walking in love and not just when others are showing you love. The true test of anyone's love is if they can give love in return for the hate received.

> Therefore be imitators of God as dear children. And walk in love as Christ also has loved us and given Himself for us; an offering and a sacrifice to God for a sweet-smelling aroma. (Ephesians 5:1–2)

> You have heard that is was said, you shall love your neighbor and hate your enemy. But I say to you, love your enemies, bless those who curse you; do good to those who hate you, and pray for those who spitefully use you and persecute you. (Matthew 5:43–44)

We must continue to remind ourselves with the scriptures that the love that must be flowing out of us to replace hate is a different kind of love. It is a level of love that can only be obtained with God's help. No man can naturally love difficult people. We tend to love the lovable and turn away from those that are difficult or who hate us. God sees hatred as evil and we can't repay evil for evil. So He asks us to love our enemies and speak a blessing over those who have spoken a curse over us. We have to pray for those that spitefully use us; and not a prayer of retaliation and destruction. God expects us to pray for their salvation and deliverance for good to come to them. What God is asking of us is to imitate the love that He had for us when He allowed His only son to die for all of us even the unlovable and difficult.

> Beloved, let us love one another, for love is of God; and everyone who loves is born of God and knows God. He who does not love does not know God; for God is love. In this the love of God was manifested toward us, that God has sent His only begotten Son into the world, that we might live through Him. In this is love, not that we loved God, but that He loved us and sent His son to be the propitiation for our sins. Beloved if God so loved us, we also ought to love one another. (1 John 4:7–11)

So often, people try to do things for God but those things are not based on love. The motive behind what is transpiring is not out of love for God or for their fellowman. The root of why such afford is made; and the responsibility it has taken is because of what onlookers will think and how they will evaluate the one providing the service. Many times, people won't participate in any type of service to others without asking the question, "What is in it for me?"

Love has to be the motivator of everything we do, otherwise, it is worthless. If we look for accolades for ourselves, those glowing words of honor spoken about your service will be the reward received. In actuality, service of any kind is not an easy endeavor because those who need the service are usually difficult because they have used this difficult behavior as a survivor mechanism. So many times, what you do may not be wanted or expected, but if it is done out of love, you will be able to withstand the difficult people and what they may take you through just so that you can provide them a service as unto God.

Though I speak with the tongues of men and of angels, but have not love I have become sounding brass or a clanging cymbal. And though I have the gift of prophecy, and understand all mysteries and all knowledge, and though I have all faith, so that I could remove mountains, but have not love, I am nothing. And though I bestow all my goods to feed the poor, and though I give my body to be burned, but have not love, it profits me nothing. Love suffers long and is kind; love does not envy; love does not parade itself, is not puffed up; does not behave rudely, does not seek its own, is not provoked, thinks no evil; does not rejoice in iniquity, but rejoices in the truth; bears all things, believes all things, hopes all things, endures all things. (1 Corinthians 13:1–7)

People don't care about what you know until they know that you care. Without love, all of our gifts and talents are valued as useless and worthless to God. He requires that we operate out of love, regardless of our position, title, or perceived anointing. I say *perceived anointing* because I question if there can be a real anointing from God if there is no love flowing from our actions. The key to any successful endeavor is love. If love is the motivator then God can make the one carrying love gifted and talented. What we need to bring to the table is our love and compassion for the people. God wants to know that we see them and care for them the way that He does, unconditionally.

CHAPTER 5

Replacing the Darkness in the Land

For darkness to be replaced, there need only be some light. Even the light from a small match can generate enough light to move darkness and reveal even a portion of what was hidden in complete darkness; so even a small light can eliminate darkness. As part of our spiritual protest, where we seek to replace darkness with light, our responsibility is to become the children of light. As children of light, it will not be what we do or say, it will be just who we are. It would be so much in our DNA that it cannot be hidden and our presence will shine a light on the darkness.

> Then Jesus spoke to them again, saying, "I am the light of the world. He who follows Me shall not walk in darkness, but have the light of life. (John 8:12)

> (Jesus says) I have come as a light into the world that whoever believes in Me should not abide in darkness. (John 12:46)

> (Jesus says) While you have the light, believe in the light that you may become sons of light. (John 12:36)

To carry light as the children of light, we have to make sure that all darkness has been eliminated from our own spirits. Meaning, we must turn from any evil hidden in us and fully submit to the idea of being image-bearers of God. To be certain that we have eliminated all evil in us, we would have to lean on God to show us who we really are and what is operating in our spirit.

> He who says he is the light and hates his brother, is in darkness until now. He who loves his brother abides in the light, and there is no cause for stumbling in him. But he who hates his brother is in darkness and walks in darkness, and does not know where he is going because the darkness has blinded his eyes. (1 John 2:9–11)

> And this is the condemnation that the light has come into the world, and men loved darkness rather than light, because their deeds were evil. For everyone practicing evil hate the light and does not come to the light, lest his deeds should be exposed. (John 3:19–20)

At one time, we all walked in darkness. We were not connected to the source of Light. Without the connection, there will be no light. Therefore, we must stay plugged into the Light to manifest the light ourselves. Light doesn't have to say anything. Light just has to be light. It is not necessary that we challenge people about their beliefs or their spiritual condition. If we are filled with the light of God, our presence is all that is needed to convict those in darkness because the light exposes. Unrighteous acts and dark devious plans will not be completed in your presence when you represent the light that exposes all darkness.

Darkness is the direct opposite of light, and the slightest amount of light can be seen in complete darkness. Light's presence provides perspective to anyone that is trying to find their way out of the darkness. Light reveals, shows the way, makes it possible to see, and it enriches. Darkness cannot pretend to be light because of its very nature. Whether someone represents darkness or light can be clearly seen.

Children of the light have the DNA of the Light of the World. One's DNA tells who created them, who gave them life, and who they are related to, it reveals the family that they belong to. In the light are peace, love, and calmness. Many fear the darkness but once there is light, the fear is gone. Things can be hidden in darkness but there is a revelation in the light. The light exposes anything hidden. In order to replace the darkness, the light must be manifested in the children of God, the children of light, not just sometimes or most of the time but all of the time.

> Let no one deceive you with empty words, for because of those things the wrath of God comes upon the sons of disobedience. Therefore do not be partakers with them; For you were once darkness but now you are light in the Lord. Walk as children of light for the fruit of the spirit is in all goodness, righteousness and truth; finding out what is acceptable to the Lord. And have no fellowship with the unfruitful works of darkness but rather expose them. For it is shameful even to speak of those things which are done by them in secret. But all things that are exposed are made manifest by the light for whatever makes manifest is light. (Eph 5:6–13)

CHAPTER 6

Replacing the Lying and Deceptive Spirit

The only way to replace lies and deception is to operate in truth. Some people feel that some situations call for *a little white lie*. But God's people, if they are going to be successful in their spiritual protest, must speak the truth regardless of the situation.

> Then Jesus said to those Jews who believed Him, "If you abide in My word, you are My disciples indeed. And you shall know the truth and the truth shall make you free." (John 8:31–32)

The truth is important to God. He hates a lie and will not accept a person that lies into His presence. As God's people come to understand the importance of being in His presence and abiding in His presence, we cannot allow a lie to take us away from God. We cannot allow a lie to hinder us from being carriers of His presence. We can't afford to come out of God's presence long enough to tell a lie.

These six things the Lord hates—yes, seven are an abomination to Him.

1. a proud look
2. a lying tongue
3. hands that shed innocent blood

4. a heart that devises wicked plans
5. feet that are swift in running to evil
6. a false witness who speaks lies
7. and one who sows discord among brethren (Proverbs 6:16–19)

Truth breaks the power of evil by displacing the lie. Our goal is not just to stop doing evil but to do good and to bear fruit for the Kingdom of God. Our goal must always be to not only cast out the evil but to fill the place it occupied with the truth of the Holy Spirit; to drive out the evil and deception with the truth. Truth is the counter-power to deception. We have to sink our roots deeper and deeper into God's truth so that it is not just a concept that we believe in but the nature of who we are.

> Lord who shall dwell [temporarily] in Your tabernacle? Who shall dwell [permanently] in Your Holy Hill? He who walks and lives uprightly and blamelessly, who works rightness and justice and speaks and thinks the truth in his heart. (Psalm 15:1–2 AMP)

We cannot be one who lies and deceives and expect to be allowed into the presence of God. Psalm 91 speaks of the secret place of God and the safety obtained by abiding in God's presence. Psalm 91:4 says He shall cover you with His feathers and under His wings, you shall take refuge; His truth shall be your shield and buckler.

The weapons of warfare that we use are not carnal but they are mighty through God to pull down the stronghold. God's truth is a defensive weapon. It is not the reality of what we see that fights the battle. It is the truth of God's Word that fights the battle.

> "And like their bow they have bent their tongues for lies. They are not valiant for the truth on the earth. For they proceed from evil to evil; and they do not know Me", says the Lord.

"Everyone take heed to his neighbor, and do not trust any brother; for every brother will utterly supplant and every neighbor will walk with slanders. Everyone will deceive his neighbor, and will not speak the truth; they have taught their tongue to speak lies; they weary themselves to commit iniquity. Your dwelling place is in the midst of deceit; through deceit they refuse to know Me," says the Lord. (Jeremiah 9:3–6)

Hear the word of the Lord, you children of Israel, for the Lord brings a change against the inhabitants of the land, There is no truth or mercy or knowledge of God in the land, By swearing and lying, killing and stealing and committing adultery, they break all restraint, with bloodshed upon bloodshed. Therefore, the land will mourn; and everyone who dwells there will waste away with the beasts of the field and the birds of the field and the birds of the air; Even the fish of the sea will be taken away. (Hosea 4:1–3)

The land now, in 2020, is in the same condition as it was in the time of Jeremiah and Hosea. Both prophets admonished the people to see how far they had traveled from God and to turn back to Him. Now God is being more specific about how to turn and what are our responsibilities to make sure that the land is healed. We must intercede not with prayer only but with a change in our lifestyle. God's people cannot continue to slumber. We must arise and be the carriers of God's presence on the earth. God's truth that we must adhere to is not only a weapon but it is also our worship. We cannot truly worship God if we don't operate in the truth of His Word; that means accepting, operating, and modifying our steps that are in direct conflict with the Word.

But the hour is coming and now is when the true worshipers will worship the Father in spirit and truth; for the Father is seeking such to worship Him. God is Spirit, and those who worship Him must worship in spirit and truth. (John 4:23–24)

As with every requirement that God places on His people, He does so knowing that we will need His help to accomplish what He requires. Jesus let his disciple know that though He had to return to heaven, the Holy Spirit was the help that He sent to provide the support needed for them to know the truth of God. That same Holy Spirit will provide us with the truth if we ask Him for help.

However, when He, the Spirit of truth, has come, He will guide you into all truth; for He will not speak on His own authority, but whatever He hears, He will speak; and He will tell you things to come. He will glorify Me, for He will take of what is Mine and declare it to you. (John 16:13–14)

Walking in the truth of God may not be the common method of operation in this day and time; however, it must be how all of God's people operate daily. We must seek after the truth and ask the Holy Spirit to lead and guide us down the path of truth.

Show me Your ways, O Lord. Teach me Your paths. Lead me in Your truth and teach me, for You are the God of my salvation; On You I wait all the day. (Psalm 25:4–5)

CHAPTER 7

Replacing Chaos and Conflict

At any given time, there is always a level of chaos and/or conflict at work. However, in 2020, there has been a massive increase due to civil and social unrest; not just in the United States but all over the world. The way to overpower chaos and conflict is to walk in peace. God's people should become peacemakers; the people that pour water on the flames of conflict. God's people should try to avoid conflicts as much as possible because we represent a God that is not part of the confusion.

> For God is not the author of confusion, but of peace, as in all churches of the saints. (1 Corinthians 14:33)

We have to see the root of confusion and chaos. We have to be aware of what is going on in the hearts and minds of those who thrive in the midst of conflict. Who would rather choose chaos than peace or would rather do battle than seek a resolution? We also have to be honest with ourselves and see if we are one of the ones that thrive in conflict and would rather do battle than seek peace.

> If you are wise and understand God's ways, prove it by living an honorable life, doing good works with the humility that comes from wis-

dom. But if you are bitterly jealous and there is selfish ambition in your heart, don't cover up the truth with boasting and lying. For jealousy and selfishness are not God's kind of wisdom. Such things are earthy, unspiritual, and demonic. For wherever there is jealousy and selfish ambition there you will find disorder and evil of every kind. But the wisdom from above is first of all pure. It is also peace loving, gentle at all times, and willing to yield to others. It is full of mercy and good deeds. It shows no favoritism and is always sincere. And those who are peacemakers will plant seeds of peace and reap a harvest of righteousness. What is causing the quarrels and fights among you? Don't they come from the evil desires at war within you? You want what you don't have, so you scheme and kill to get it. You are jealous of what others have, but you can't get it, so you fight and wage war to take it away from them. Yet you don't have what you want because you don't ask God for it. And even when you ask you don't get it because your motives are all wrong—you want only what will give you pleasure. (James 3:13–14:3 NLT)

If what is operating inside of us is from God, we will find it easy to be a peacemaker. But, if what is inside of us is not from God there will be no peace around us because there is no peace inside of us. Being a person that operates as a peacemaker is against our natural human impulses. Therefore, in order to successfully operate as a peacemaker, a person would need a source that changes their very nature. That strong force with the ability to change our nature is God. He is the only power that can successfully change us. We can't easily escape conflict because we are all products of our own misguided desires. We are all part of the problem and the problem is part of all of us. All of us say and do self-motivated, self-centered things that trigger conflict; that is why we have to turn to God to change our nature.

The Bible gives us instructions on how to deal with conflict. I remember when first reading these scriptures; I thought, *God can't be serious. Who can do this?* But I soon found out that God was serious. I have also found out that when things are too hard for us to do in our own strength, we only need to ask God for His help and He will help us to do it.

> But I say to you who hear: Love your enemies; do good to those who hate you; bless those who curse you; and pray for those who spitefully use you. To him who strikes you on the one cheek, offer the other also. And from him who takes away your cloak, do not withhold your tunic either. Give to everyone who ask of you. And from him who takes away your goods do not ask them back. And just as you want men to do to you, you also do to them likewise. But if you love those who love you what credit is that to you? For even sinners love those who love them. And if you do good to those who do good to you, what credit is that to you? For even sinners do the same. And if you lend to those from who you hope to receive back, what credit is that to you? For even sinners lend to sinners to receive as much back. But love your enemies, do good, and lend, hoping for nothing in return; and your reward will be great, and you will be sons of the Most High; for He is kind to the unthankful and evil. Therefore be merciful, just as your Father also is merciful. (Luke 6:27–36)

Jesus spoke these words to make it very clear as to how God expected His children to behave in the midst of conflict. Peacemakers use conflict as an opportunity to solve problems in a way that not only benefits everyone involved but also honors God; Peacemakers use conflict to glorify God, serve others, and become more like Christ. Proverbs 12:20 refers to these individuals as counselors of peace that will have joy.

> Great peace have those who love Your law, and nothing causes them to stumble. (Psalms 119:65)

> Depart from evil and do good; seek peace and pursue it. (Psalms 34:14)

Jesus left us peace and told the disciples before He had gone to the cross, that we could have peace. He also said, expect tribulations in this world but pursue peace because He had already overcome the spirits operating in the world. Jesus understood that when He would die and rise from the dead, He would obtain victory over all of the enemy's tactics and scheme. Jesus assured the disciples and spoke these words even before He had been betrayed and arrested. He knew the assignment and what needed to be done on His part so that we would and could do our part now, at this end-time. We have to know that our peace is in Him. He won that peace for us when He not only died on the cross but He rose from death.

> Peace I leave with you, My peace I give to you; not as the world gives do I give to you. Let not your heart be troubled, neither let it be afraid. (John 14:27)

> These things I have spoken to you, that in Me you may have peace. In the world you will have tribulation; but be of good cheer, I have overcome the world. (John 16:33)

So God expects us to serve Him in peace. It doesn't speak well of His children to be out of control and involved in chaos and conflict. His DNA in us should manifest His character in situations of conflict. Paul expressed this requirement to the Roman church. It was not a recommendation or a suggestion; it was what is expected of us. We serve God when we operate in righteousness, peace, and joy, especially when our situation may not dictate that response. When our character in the worse times manifests peace and joy, God is honored.

> For the kingdom of God is not eating and drinking, but righteousness and peace and joy in the Holy Spirit. For he who serves Christ in these things is acceptable to God and approved by men. Therefore, let us pursue the things which make for peace and the things by which one may edify another. (Rom 14:17–19)

Though our lives before we accepted Jesus Christ as Lord and Savior may not have been peaceful, we all have the opportunity, regardless of our past, to connect with the creator of peace. All we have to do is seek Him for help. His word gives us no excuses or allowances for continuing in chaos and conflict. We have to be obedient to what the word is telling us about peace. We have to trust God that if we hold our peace, He will fight our battle.

> Let your gentleness be known to all men. The Lord is at hand. Be anxious for nothing, but in everything, by prayer and supplication, with thanksgiving, let your requests be made known to God; and the peace of God, which surpasses all understanding will guard you hearts and minds through Christ Jesus. (Philippians 4–7)

> Pursue peace with all people, and holiness, without which no one will see the Lord; looking carefully, lest anyone fall short of the grace of God; lest any root of bitterness springing up

cause trouble, and by this many become defiled. (Hebrews 12:14–15)

Finally, all of you be of one mind; having compassion for one another; love as brother, be tenderhearted, be courteous, not returning evil for evil or reviling for reviling, but on the contrary blessing, knowing that you were called to this; that you may inherit a blessing; for he who would love life and see good days, let him refrain his tongue from evil, and his lips from speaking deceit. Let him turn away from evil and do good. Let him seek peace and pursue it; for the eyes of the Lord are on the righteous and His ears are open to their prayers. But the face of the Lord is against those who do evil. (1 Peter 3:8–12)

CHAPTER 8

Maintaining Your Place in the Presence of God

The process to get in the presence of God will not be the hardest part of this journey. Where we will encounter the most challenges will be to maintain a place in the presence of God. We must never underestimate the enemy of our soul. The devil will never give up on trying to take us back to the starting line or even farther back than the starting line. He will throw anything at you to get you to pick up hate again, to get you attached to darkness, to get you to lie or deceive someone, or to get you involved in some kind of conflict.

He is relentless and we should also be relentless for the things of God. As hard as you fight to stay in God's presence, the harder the enemy tries to oppose our efforts. But God has provided us with a safe place. God has revealed to me that to stay in God's presence, we have to find the secret place of the Bible in Psalm 91. That secret place is being in Christ. If we are in Christ, He is surrounding us. We are in Him and He is our refuge.

The secret place—why is this place that we need to be in God a secret? Most things that are secret are intentionally hidden from the masses. It is also not easily found. But God is not hiding the secret place from us. In fact, the map to this secret place is right in the scripture that talks about this place of safety.

> He who dwells in the secret place of the Most High shall remain stable and fixed under the shadow of the Almighty [Whose power no foe can withstand]. I will say of the Lord, He is my Refuge and my Fortress, my God; on Him I lean and rely, and in Him I [confidently] trust. For [then] He will deliver you from the snare of the fowler and from the deadly pestilence. [Then] He will cover you with His pinions, and under His wings shall you trust and find refuge; His truth and His faithfulness are a shield and a buckler. You shall not be afraid of the terror of the night; nor of the arrow (the evil plots and slanders of the wicked) that flies by day. Nor of the pestilence that stalks in darkness; nor of the destruction and sudden death that surprise and lay waste at noonday. A thousand may fall at your side, and ten thousand at your right hand, but it shall not come near you. Only a spectator shall you be [yourself inaccessible in the secret place of the Most High] as you witness the reward of the wicked. Because you have made the Lord you refuge, and the Most high your dwelling place, there shall no evil befall you; nor any plague or calamity come near your tent; For He will give His angels [especial] charge over you to accompany and defend and preserve you in all your ways [of obedience and service]. (Psalms 91:1–11 AMP)

These six factors are highlighted to me as I read and meditate on this scripture. I believe these six factors outline how to get to and remain stable and fixed in that secret place.

- Remain stable and fixed under the shadow of the Almighty.
- He is my refuge and my fortress.
- In Him will I trust.
- His truth shall be my shield and buckler.
- I shall not be afraid.
- I will make the Lord my dwelling place (my habitation).

Remain Stable and Fixed under the Shadow of the Almighty

The practice and motivation of many of God's people are that in ministry, they want their name to be great. They want to be recognized and seen by others. There is a focus on their anointing and their ministry. However, if we abide in the shadow, we are not seen. A shadow is a dark area or shape produced by a body coming between rays of light and a surface. The Almighty, our God, our Lord is the body. He is the surface and we are the shape produced as the light shines on Him. When ministry is done right, God gets the glory. The light is on Him and He is the one that gets the attention.

The Almighty is what is seen and we are hidden. Our flesh hates not being seen. It enjoys being acknowledged and recognized. Expect the enemy to try and sneak in pride as you minister. Expect the enemy to try to get you to move out of the shadow into the forefront. But the secret place is in the shadow. We must be the reflection of God, a shadow of Him, to be stable and fixed in the secret place.

God is My Refuge and Fortress

A refuge and fortress is a building that is entered into when a person is in trouble or in the midst of a fight. The purpose of entering into the fortress is to have added protection, away from the elements, and not be so available and reachable to the enemy. This factor reminds me of the benefits of being in Christ. Being in Christ and entering into God for refuge and fortress have the same benefits. As we enter into battle with the enemy and he tries to draw us out of the protection of God; we must stay in God and remind ourselves and the enemy of these benefits:

- We are justified; made upright, placed in right standing with God (Romans 3:24).
- We are freed from condemnation and guilt (Romans 8:1–2).
- We cannot be separated from the love of God (Romans 8:39).
- We are part of the Body of Christ (Romans 12:5).
- We are consecrated and purified; made holy; selected to be His people (1 Corinthians 1:2).
- We are lead daily by God; we are His trophies from the victory of Christ (1 Corinthians 2:14–15).
- We are a new creation (2 Corinthians 5:17).
- We are reconciled to God and given the ministry of reconciling others to Christ. (2 Corinthians 5:18).
- We are sons of God (Galatians 3:26–28).
- We are blessed with every spiritual blessing in the heavenly realm (Ephesians 1:3).
- We are made alive and in union with Christ; we are delivered from judgment and made partakers of Christ's salvation; we have joint seating with Christ in the heavenly sphere (Ephesians 2:5–6).

Let me be clear that being a Christian does not necessarily mean that you are in Christ unless you are conforming to His Word and taking advantage of the benefits. The one thing God makes clear throughout His Word is that we can't enter into His presence bringing any and everything with us. We have to truly become a new creature with a new mindset to enter into God's presence.

In Him Will I Trust

Trusting in God should be the first option. It should never be what we turn to after trying all of our options based on our own reasoning. Our trust in God should not be situational. It should not be restricted or limited. It should be what we will to do even when we don't particularly like the outcome or understand the reason for the outcome. Trusting God is an act of our will. Trusting Him to lead, direct, and control our life. Trust God to get you to the paths that He has predestined for you to walk on. Too often, we trust God to help during times of trouble but how much trouble could we have avoided if we sought God and trusted God to help in the initial decision? Many bad decisions will be prevented. Victory would be secured and blessings assured.

His Truth Shall Be My Shield and Buckler

A shield is a weapon used as protection against blows or missiles. A buckler is a smaller round shield worn on the forearm used in hand-to-hand combat. God's truth is what He says in His Word. His truth is the weapon used to protect against blows or missiles. God's truth is also used in close combat with the enemy. The truth of God is that no weapon formed against us shall prosper (Isaiah 54:17). That truth lets us know that a weapon may be formed and used but it will not accomplished what it was sent out to do. We are protected. It is not the reality of what you see that fights the battle; it is not what you think that fights the battle; it is the truth of God's Word—the truth of the last thing He spoke to you regardless of what is seen by your natural eye. His truth has to be the main emphasis. We must, in turn, speak the truth, render the truth, and judge truthfully.

I Shall Not Be Afraid

> God has not given us the spirit of fear but of power, and of love, and of a sound mind. (2 Timothy 1:7)

Fear is a tool of the devil. It is the open door that he uses to paralyze and hinder our movement. When we cooperate with fear, by allowing it to take over our spirit, fear will direct what steps we take. When fear directs our steps, it takes away our destiny. It takes away our God-given purpose and power. It stops us from operating in love because we can't be fearful and also operate in love. Love is selfless where fear is always expecting someone to take advantage of us or misuse us.

In fear, we fight the divine connection and relationships that God has predestined in our lives. Fear makes our minds weak. Fear can cause us to be double-minded. Fear can also make it difficult for us to walk in faith and trust God for the things that have not yet been manifested in the natural realm. We cannot be afraid, but we must lean on and trust in God at every turn in our lives. We have to know and not doubt that He has us and that He never leaves us.

Make the Lord My Habitation, My Dwelling Place

A habitation and a dwelling place are synonymous. They both mean the state or process of living in a particular place. Living in the Lord is the perfect place. It is the secret place where we are not seen by the enemy and cannot be reached by the enemy. When the enemy looks for us, all he sees is God. It is why a thousand may fall at our side and ten thousand at our right hand but we will only be a spectator, not affected. There is a promise of inaccessibility that exists in the secret place of the Most High. The enemy would have himself come through God to get to us and if he does come through God, he himself would be changed, delivered, and set free. The enemy knows that he cannot get that close to God.

The identity of a spectator takes away all the stress and pressure associated with any situation or event. It is like watching a movie and during the tense and dangerous portion, you'll feel a little kick of excitement but not much because you know you are really not a part of what is occurring on the screen. In our lives, we are spectating and watching what God will do in our lives and the way of escape He will provide when needed. There is no fear because of the trust we have in the Lord that we live in.

CONCLUSION

This book serves as both a challenged to grow in God and an invitation to participate in standing in the gap for this world. God's desire is that everyone would come to know Him and be saved from the outcome that was prepared for the devil. However, as the body of Christ slept at our post, the world has gotten into a place of great darkness where great intercession is needed. We must be willing to fight this battle God's way. The easier it is for us to release our will over to God, the easier it will be to take this journey that God pre-determined for us.

The scriptures bear it out that what God is trying to get us on board with is His end-time plan to gather in those who don't yet know Him and His power. The attitude and mindset developed on this journey must be held to and must become a part of the fabric of our makeup. It should be not only what we do but who we are. We can only maintain our position in God when we stay in the secret place that is accessible to us, God's people, yet hidden from the enemy. God is calling us to bring His kingdom to the earth with miracles, signs, and wonders following.

May God bless and keep you as you accept the invitation and the challenge to be the intercessor that heals the land with our lives, our prayers, and our declarations. May we continue to be empowered to be the Atmosphere Changers that will positively effect change in this world.

ABOUT THE AUTHOR

Diane White was born and raised in Oakland, California. She has been married for thirty-seven years and is the mother of two sons and grandmother of twelve. She retired as a corporate auditor from the federal government. She earned a bachelor of science in accounting, a doctorate in Christian counseling, and recently received her board certification as a master mental health coach.

Diane, along with her husband, founded the Tree of Life Restoration Ministries, where she serves as pastor, and Extending a Hand Community Outreach Mission, Inc., a nonprofit organization where she serves as a counselor for the counseling center and instructor for the leadership development courses. She works part-time for Sister to Sister dba (doing business as) Serenity House, a women's dual diagnosis drug recovery program. There she is the program director and is responsible for counseling and teaching groups in anger management and recovery from domestic violence. She is also the founder of Sarah's Daughters, a nonprofit organization whose goal is to empower women in every area of their lives.

CPSIA information can be obtained
at www.ICGtesting.com
Printed in the USA
BVHW040308210721
612415BV00018B/1596